THIS UNCOMMON SOLITUDE

Pandemic Poetry from the Pacific Northwest

THIS UNCOMMON SOLITUDE

Pandemic Poetry from the Pacific Northwest

Sidekick Press
Bellingham, Washington

Published 2020
Printed in the United States of America
ISBN 978-1-7344945-4-9
LCCN 2020943061

Sidekick Press
2950 Newmarket Street
Suite 101-329
Bellingham, WA 98226
https://sidekickpress.com

This Uncommon Solitude: Pandemic Poetry from the Pacific Northwest

Cover Design: Spoken Designs – spokendesigns.com
Cover Photograph: Sasha Freemind
Back Cover Art: C.J. Prince
Title Credit: Drue (BeDo) Robinson

DEDICATION

This book is dedicated to all of us
as we rise to the challenges
that deepen us, bring us together, and
teach us to value one another
more wisely than we did before.

CONTENTS

INTRODUCTION

This Uncommon Solitude captures the myriad and diverse experiences of Red Wheelbarrow Writers during these times of quarantine and the COVID-19 pandemic. We reach out to connect, but we can't physically touch each other. We are shaken by news of widespread suffering and death caused by a novel virus that inexorably spirals out of control. We feel powerless and isolated. Ongoing catastrophes of racism and environmental decline trouble our hearts. For many of us, poetry has helped connect us, one to another, as we share experiences and insights, express our grief and sadness, fears and pain, gratitude and hope. In joining together, we feel our way forward as best we can toward making sense of our transformed world.

The Red Wheelbarrow Writers group hosts a virtual community of writers bearing witness to this viral isolation, these unfolding crises, through words and images, emotions and spirit. We see our role as chroniclers and interpreters of these unprecedented times. In exquisite detail and broad concept, our words convey anguish and hope, power and humor, despair and loveliness. We hope each poem brings to you, as it has to us, the exceptional gift of connection during this time of isolation and change.

Susan Chase-Foster, Victoria Doerper, and Joe Nolting, Editors on behalf of Red Wheelbarrow Writers, Autumn 2020

I'M HERE. NOTHING ELSE TO DO.
by Red Wheelbarrow Writers Collective

These empty streets,
Stores closed up
The urban silence
Magnifies birdsong.

Sequestered
In pandemic
I'm longing
For my grandkids.

Dogwood flowers
Perched atop branches
Alter my perception.
Time has utterly changed
And a day is as long
As a heartbeat.

I sense urgency
But nothing I can do.

Gratitude. I'm still here.

Out of balance
Sleep patterns,
Moods change,
And I feel useless...
One long writing retreat,
Nothing else I can do.

One siren a day.
Eagle and hawk forage
While crows scream.
My life is fluid
Like dropping acid
Hard to read
And I don't get dressed.

Going downhill fast
This grim pandemic spring
A dollop of despair...

Frantic people
Throw things into carts
You're masked
You can't see faces
My body floats
In an ocean
Of disconnection.
But forest colors are vibrant.

The border is closed
Rabbits sit on my front porch
Juxtaposition
Grateful and vulnerable
I'm just here.

DUSK IN THE GARDEN
by Susan Chase-Foster

Possibly a coronavirus
With a penchant for fevers
Is heating things up,
Or spring has, at last,
Sashayed into our garden.
Ponder the kinnikinnick
Popcorning pink blossoms
From their stacked stone bed,
The gang of gray squirrels
Mining what remains
Of filberts from cedar boxes
of arugula, and above,
In our Douglas fir a chorus
Of crows cackling a Steller's jay
Away from their nest.
Regard two golden spirals
Of snail resting on a laurel leaf,
And the wine-red woodlouse spider
Waddling through a sea of moss,
Her egg bulb bobbing like a buoy,
The arsenal of purple hosta spears
Stabbing their way through the earth,
And the cosmos of buttercups
Tossing constellations of yellow stars
Across the lawn.
Consider how in the darkening sky
An orb of immense illumination ascends,
Beholds us like the silver Eye of God,
Fills us with hope.

A HISTORY OF CORONA, n.
by Linda Lambert

If I could write a shape poem
like George Herbert's *Altar*
or a 4th grader's versified rainbow
I would, but searing coronavirus
TV images of grainy grey balls,
spiked and pierced by red thorns,
do not lend themselves to
decorative constructs.

Instead, I heed the advice of
Miss Virginia Smith,
high school Latin teacher:
Learn the origin of words,
she said, 50% of English
comes from Latin.

And Miss Lucille Bertheau,
8th grade English teacher:
Read a book. Find five new words.
Use each in a sentence.

I credit them both with habits
delivering amusement and learning.
Plagued as the world is with the specter
of illness, I am lifted by the fanciful,
practical, scientific, and surprising
applications (discounting Mexican
beer and Cuban branded cigars)
of a word like corona.

Corona, coronae's earliest associations:
　　　wreathes of flowers,
　　　circlets of gold, chaplets,
　　　and a monarch's crown.

E. Phillips' 1658 definition in
The New World of Eng. Words:
　　　"a small circle of light,
　　　(usually prismatically colored)
　　　appearing round the sun and moon,
　　　also...an anthelion, *n.*"

Astronomy
　　　"the halo of radiating white light
　　　seen around the disco of the moon
　　　in a total eclipse of the sun."

　　　"corona australis, corona borealis:
　　　two constellations, the Southern and
　　　Northern Crown, consisting
　　　of elliptical rings of stars."

Religion
　　　"a circular chandelier suspended from
　　　the roof of a church; more fully
　　　Corona lucis (crown of light)."

　　　"the tonsure of a cleric." [Mediaeval
　　　Latin *corona clericalis*] "The shaving
　　　of the head or part of it as a religious
　　　practice or rite, esp. as a preparation
　　　to entering the priesthood..."

Architecture
> "a member of cornice, above the
> bed-moulding and below the
> cymatium, having a broad vertical face."

Botany
> "an appendage on the top of a seed, as
> the pappus on that of a dandelion
> or thistle."

Pathology
> "syphilitic blotches on the forehead,
> which often extend around it like
> a crown."

1968: in *Nature* magazine, eight virologists
> suggested that "a previously unrecognized
> group of viruses...should be called
> coronaviruses."

So here we are, besotted with news,
in a state of adjustment and wait,
my future learning and amusement
delivered by words left undefined:
chaplets, anthelion, bed-moulding,
and cymatium.

Definition source: Oxford English Dictionary

ANOTHER TRAIN
by Gary Wade

Another train
like the train before
rattles darkness and
silence of the city,
calls for its crossings
and leaves
shards of irritation
for folk balanced
on the cusp
of wakefulness and sleep.

THE LEAST OF THE LEAST
by Carol McMillan

A little string of nucleotides
A billion times smaller than a spider's eyelash
Creeps through the humans
Using each one to make
another trillion copies of itself.

Unmoved
Uncaring
Unfeeling
Unknowing
Not even living

Just a tiny string of nucleotides
In a certain order
Changing the world.

UNEMPLOYED
by Joy Wright

March 16th schools closed
no work for substitutes
look for a new job
something else temporary
using compassion but fear
keeps me logging in,
to complete my weekly claim.
Able to work? Seeking work?
Completing job searches?
Impacted by COVID-19?
I peck away at the keys
hoping my appeal will
be settled soon because
I missed that question
previously, the one
requesting I upload
proof of identity. So,
for now unemployed
with no income.

TOILET PAPER
by JK Small

Searching the shelves in stores
For toilet paper
All gone

Searching the shelves
For Vitamin C
All gone

Searching the shelves
For hydrogen peroxide
All gone

Since when in our abundant country
Are stores empty of these items
Since COVID-19
Has arrived

As shoppers hoard these items
To stay safe

Everyone is looking out for themselves
We hunker down at home
Waiting for toilet paper to arrive

We ask our neighbors
If they have an extra roll of toilet paper
That they could put in a bag and leave at our door

Good Grief

Of all things to need the most
Toilet Paper

SIDEWALK DANCE
by Rebecca Mabanglo-Mayor

Purple
phlox in
full bloom rock
to rhythms set
by spring
breezes
while
daring squirrels
steal food left
for nesting crows
who caw
distress.

PLUNDER
by Joe Nolting

I will not become a hoarder
not stockpile sacks of flour
cans of beans
bottles of bleach
rolls of toilet paper.

I will not become a pirate
not pillage the grocer's shelves
to seize the pandemic's
precious plunder, as if I could
build a ship from these items
sail on an ocean of calm
to a world free of disease.

But today I navigate
the store's perilous waters
paper mask as life raft
float past other shoppers
adrift on the breaking waves
of our collective nightmare.

I follow my treasure map
ease into the sheltered cove
of greeting cards, where only
two items remain, identical
sympathy cards, one of which I need
the other I suddenly covet
until I sense a fellow traveler
treading water six feet away
watching me, weighing
the value of my plunder.

TO BE BRAVE by Judith Shantz

Chalk art in a rounded hand,
a child's hand,
spells *courage* on the pavement...
be brave, be strong...
in pastel shades of
sun
and shadow

But strength is not the same
as bravery.
It is one thing
to plant your feet and lean
into the hurricane
when there is
no recourse
but hanging on

It's quite another thing to walk,
chin up, high-headed,
proud and even
confident
to face the lion
in its den

I yelp in pain
before the blow is felt.
I check the falling sky.
Not the chicken-little sky,
but all its falling shoes
tumbling unexpectedly
into this graveyard of steel-toed boots,
piled up for years—
each one a grief
or loss.

This now, in my old age,
my craven
litany.
Infirmity, irrelevance,
decay.
A tiny microbe fashioned as
a medieval mace.
The looming loss
of my own
small,
sweet light

My lover, warm and restless,
coughs in the night—
dry and rasping
and I wake,
a damp prickle of fear
along my hairline;
the hot rush that threatens to
disembowel me

Maybe next year I'll be brave.

ADVICE by Victoria Doerper

Yesterday I had a conversation
With a fellow morning walker.
She and I always say hello,
Stand close on the gravel path
And briefly chat, though now
We physically separate ourselves,
Walk on the street in distant parallel,
Footprints never threading together.
We talked about sewing machines,
An odd topic since neither of us
Has skill or experience sewing.
She's full of energy and intention
And has already taught herself
To make masks on her new machine.
I bought a portable, I say,
But I won't get it until next week.
I plan to make face masks too.
OK, she advises, let me tell you this:
Pay attention to the needle.
Not the thread? I ask. Not the fabric?
Well, mostly, she says, it's the needle.
How strong it is.
Whether it can push through
And come back out again
Without breaking.
Uh oh, I think, and realize I have no idea
How to handle myself in this new milieu.
Anything else? I ask.
One more really important thing, she says,
You have to manage the tension
So the thread won't break,
So when you're done,
Everything is still intact.
So you can start again
And make something new.

HOW TO MEASURE DURING A PANDEMIC
by Nancy Canyon

Start with a body reference—say the distance
between index finger and thumb; use a
ruler to establish a 6- to 7-inch segment.

Accuracy is not the point. The estimate
of space is not meant to be precise—
just a convenience.

The implement of measurement
is always with you. It can be easily doubled,
by placing both hands together.

This is how I measure the fabric and two
pieces of elastic I use to make a facemask.
The distance I must keep from another—

something I never imagined necessary—
can be ascertained by reaching my arms out
to the sides. The length from fingertip

to fingertip equals my height: 5 ½-feet.
If you remember *height=distance* (give
or take a little) relief becomes obvious:

you are here, and they are there. No more
guesswork as to the 6-feet of separation
one must maintain during a pandemic.

BENEATH THE PINK MOON
by Betty Scott

I swear:
I refuse
to live out
the rest of my life
like a *Dryocopus pileatus,*
ramming my beak
against the bark
of techno realities.

At least that is what
I tell myself
before I turn on
my computer
to see what the hell
I've missed.

HORI HORI by Susan Chase-Foster

Mostly, I avoid
Overthinking the virus
By flicking slugs
Off hostas,
Uprooting buttercups
And ivy with my
Hori hori knife,
By ambling
Through alleys
An hour a day,
Baking anything
With sugar,
Drinking anything
With alcohol,
Writing poem
After poem.
But last night,
An armada
Of round-crowned
Antagonists
Floated as red mist
Into my dream,
Delivered
A momentary drowse
Of nightmarish
Disorientation
Until I rallied,
Ripped my hori hori
From its sheath,
Whipped the mist
With my magic blade,
Knocked off
Their killer coronas,
And sent them back
To hell
Where they belong.

MICROCORONA
by Elizabeth Tervo

The world is tamed now, small:
housewife's work of dishes and on-time meals
(still Lenten until someone tells me otherwise)
and garden, cleaning, letters and quiet time.

Like when you have a newborn baby
and life shuts down to meals and sleep
sometimes you manage to send out a photo
that brings a smile.

Outside the danger particles swarm,
twisted crownlets settling down on cardboard,
on metal, on food, on people...
and streaming through the ether
blue masks, blue faces, blue police.

Some people's whole purpose in life
is to warn us of the danger and to fight it.
Mine is to say I went for a walk
and I saw a pretty flower.

ON THE FIELD
by Joy Wright

From the announcers' booth I can see
it will be a glorious day in the park
the mowers are running in tandem
the line painters freshening home plate
that will hopefully need a dusting soon.
The empty stands shine with morning dew
dancing with anticipation of roaring
stomping fans. Which young local voice
will belt out the anthem? Which mascot will
lead the cheers today? Which sponsors
will give something away?
From the announcers' booth, I can't see
the empty parking lot and the ticket
booth latched and locked. I can't see
the yellow caution tape or the 'closed
due to COVID-19' safety sign. I can't see
the players at home with their families or
the fans tossing balls in their own yards.

WALKING TOGETHER
by Cami Ostman

I went for a walk with an old friend.
We kept our distance.
Six feet apart
Except when we forgot
And drifted together
Like egg yolks
In an old, uneven frying pan.

Once, yesterday, I even touched his arm
As I might normally do when sharing a joke,
Feeling warm.
And then I remembered
He might be able to kill me.
I might kill him too.
This will be hard to remember.

PREVENTION LAPSE
by Carol McMillan

Don't touch, don't touch
Don't touch, don't touch, don't touch!
Wipe it down, wipe it down,
Wipe it down, wipe it down, wipe it down!
There–could–be–virus–anywhere...

Shelter at home, shelter at home,
Touch no one.
Be touched by nothing except this
Profound pandemic paranoia.

In a wild act of rebellion
I gleefully touch my face and rub my eyes.

THE LONGEST SPRING
by C.J. Prince

A cup of Earl Grey warms my hands
as I rock and gaze at shifting light
in the garden and wonder of the future.

Elsewhere, a frigerator truck
eases down the back alley
of a hospital—

a semi full of bodies,
stacked like mangled books,
a plague in progress.

Even looking northwest
to see hyacinths' heavy heads, rain weary,
I feel a dirge of funerals in my blood—

worried sorrow lest someone is misplaced.
Bodies long ago lost at Bayview Cemetery.
Today how can it not happen again?

Winter's departure and we grit our teeth
at signs of spring, the hapless herald of hope,
pointing out narcissus blooms

that cannot hide a virus.
COVID-19 points our way,
a spotlight to dodge.

We are nobody today, nor yesterday,
upper case Truth or lower case,
any day, any month or any year,

alive or not living,
death dawdles along to tend last rites.
Looking out my window, I rock,

feeling the comfort of the wood-burning stove.
The cat is on and off my shoulder.
Only I wonder

if there will be a morning.
If I had to see it to believe it,
I wouldn't believe hummingbird wings

hovering at an empty hook.
I make sugar water for the feeder.
Who knows but the world may end tonight.

SANCTUARY
by Janet Oakley

Cautiously, I step into my garden,
Imaging a summer's feast of beans and greens.
A chickadee chats its carefree song.
In this space, I am free
Until the storm is over.

CORVID
by Marian Exall

I keep mis-saying COVID,
Although the word crops up
A dozen times a day.
Instead of a pandemic,
I think of crows
Picking at spilled garbage,
Heads tilted, feet dancing.

Crow's feet: my face
In the mirror.
Newly old, "vulnerable;"

The president crowing
Over the market's surge
While unemployment soars;

A murder of crows—
The police line clad
In battledress
Advances.

A new world
With a new word
I cannot master.
I can only stay
Out of the way.

SLIDING GLASS DOOR REVIEW
by C.J. Prince

As darkness sneaks into cedar roots,
a fire flickers in the windowpane,
turnabout images muted in starlight.
Daylight reveals rain and dirt stains,
an off-kilter screen
and last year's dusty cobwebs.

A fine window to observe
a panorama of a pandemic.
The marmalade cat, still as a stone,
a wavering Egyptian Bast,
leaps, disturbing some undefined
symmetry of space.
The blotchy oilcloth table
piled with stacks of papers,
jars of paintbrushes, turpentines,
and gambols, oils and acrylics,

the centerpieces, unseen in window reflection,
unseen at eye level, lost in the jumble
of tarot decks, a stack of last month's
Wall Street Journals, a single horizon line
mirrored in the windowpane.

In the multi-dimensional,
a soft eye looks through a glass darkly,
spikes of hostas emerge like incense sticks
from an invisible pot.

A dining chair disabled from sight,
only a stripe of white sticky tape
to deter feline claws.
The orange cat, the only cat,
the shadow of a cat,
the investigator within
these four walls,
the one who re-sniffs
each of two dozen
paint brushes
for an unrevealed clue,
that cat, who has not noticed
the quilting project under the blank
empty day planner,
or the roll of scotch tape,
hand cream or ephemeris.
The images will shift at dawn,
When a sun thunders through the forest
To poke at this reviewer's eyes of sleep.
It will look all the same
but different—

Different as the big leaf maple,
catkins twisting dance, rain battered,
now to tiny leaves, shining
through a sun break.
This sliding glass door,
Only a windowful of change
and wonder, only a passing
breath of pollen,
only a moment,
in a pandemic.

IN OUR MINDS, WE ARE ALREADY GONE
by Kate Miller

Tonight I'm awake again, early morning,
buoyed by the lonely comfort of trains
whistle-rattling through late night towns. In a
darkness somehow darker than before, I know
these trains carry the freight of things, not
lives. Though engine crews still ride these
midnight trains, essential workers in a newly
perilous world, the cars are empty of human
freight, carry no grandparents traveling to meet
their grandchildren, no college kids returning
after spring break, no young couples moving
cross-country, no tourists come to see melting
glaciers and hump-backed whales, no human
cargo vulnerable to viruses. Only material goods
traverse our country now, cars heavy with food
and fuel and stuff of lives, absent its citizens, who
lie alone in their beds at home, small in their
static selves, chafing to return to the wider
world. We are all restless, awake, listening.
Wheels rattle on tracks, horns blow blues riffs,
car after car bumping through the backyards of
our dreams, escaping town without us again.

ON READING EDUARDO C. CORRAL
by Susan Chase-Foster

Wandering along the shadow side
of Mt. Pandemic, I came across
a portal of words that led me out
of death-black darkness.

Some Mesoamerican elders
believed there's a fifth direction.

Not the sky or the ground
but the person right next to you.

Poets, we are in this together.
Your poem speaks next to mine,
mine next to yours. May our words
be glowing portals of light and life.

WASHING HANDS by Victoria Doerper

It began as battle,
The twenty second
Skirmish with a wily foe,
An engagement
Maybe twenty
Or thirty times a day,
Fighting an enemy
Trying to turn me
Into a weapon
Against myself.
Then the cracked skin,
The burning backs of hands
Until the routine
Of lotion and cream
Brought epidermal
Salvation.

I find odd comfort now
In soap and water,
Juxtaposition of
"Happy Birthday"
With fear of death
While I work
A smooth lather
Between fingers,
My fans of knuckles
Coming together,
Brother-bones to brothers,
Remembering their kinship.
I'm surprised by tenderness
In the feel of hollowed
Hand around thumb,
The perfect fit of fingertips
In open palm,
The washing away,
The hallowed anointing.

GROCERY SHOPPING NOW
by Laura Rink

The list on the fridge:
Coronavirus surface-survival rates.

Attire: Mask, required. Gloves, optional.
Hand sanitizer in pocket. Credit card in pocket.
Wear clothes with pockets.

Procure cart from clean side of foyer.
Watch exiting shopper push empty cart
toward you. Not here! You gesture
wildly. There! Dirty side.

Enter and pause.
Assess prevailing travel patterns.
Insert yourself into circuitous flow
of produce section.

All those people you
ignored as you dashed around
grabbing items on your list
in the Before Times?

Be hyperaware of their
positions. Their lingering,
their surges.
Prepare for reversals.

Peer at use-by-dates.
Touch only what you'll take.
Hear your mother say
take only what you'll eat.

Take only what you are
prepared to disinfect.
Minimize refrigerated items
that must be cleaned immediately.

Avoid the talkative cashier
not wearing a mask.
Hit your mark in line, and
advance six feet at a time.

Home.
Car trunk—
A holding station for pantry items.
Pile bags on "dirty" counter.

Argue with partner, not terribly but exhaustively,
debating proper cleaning procedures,
setting up an assembly line—bag to fridge.

Strip—clothes and mask into
washing machine, body into shower.

Grocery shopping complete.

HOPE TRANSFORMS
by Nancy Canyon

We have you on the run, and to think you still
call us beautiful—like a flower—or maybe your own DNA
enlarged beneath a microscope. But really, we are as scared as
you are, not ugly threats from a wet market, but space dust
randomly landing on a strange planet: homeless, hungry, no
one stepping up to show us the ropes. You are warm and
energetic, the perfect petri dish. Give us a chance and we will
both be transformed—see the headline: COVID GOES HOME.

AUBADE WITH VIRUS
by Victoria Doerper

The robin wakes me
With cheerful song
Before the light comes up,
Before my conscious mind
Reminds me that today
Is not a normal day
And I do not inhabit
My month-ago world.
There is coffee to drink,
News to read,
Strange thoughts to think,
Dark feelings to feel.
My morning walk
Now takes
Hypervigilance,
Turns my mind
From blossoming trees
And worm-pulling birds
To a narrow gravel path
Booby-trapped
By heedless people
Pushing close enough
To brush me with sickness
Or death.

I am angry and afraid,
Though the trees and birds
Counsel calm. Remember,
They seem to say,
Threat has always ridden
On the back of a flea,
Wings of a hawk,

Gnawing jaws of a beetle,
Trophy hunter's bloodied hands,
A breath of air.
The world has always been
Dangerous,
And still we
Awaken to the early light,
Set buds,
Flutter and trill,
Go on with our day
In an uncertain world
That is not un-beautiful.

HOW THEN SHALL WE LIVE
by Cheryl Nelson

We heard that people died.
People in other countries:
Spain, Italy, China, South Korea.
People unknown to us.
We must know.
Some not remembered.
We must remember
Brothers, sisters,
Mothers, fathers,
Friends, lovers.
Say their names.

We care for the sick,
Take them dinner,
Talk with them on the phone,
Email, Facetime, TikTok, text.
We long for connection.
Let us connect.

We grieve.
Oh, how we grieve,
Bodies shaking,
Voices keening,
Inconsolable tears,
Together we cry.

Restless and lonely,
We impatiently wait
For normal to return,
To have life be
What it used to be,
Our familiar life.

Normal again?
Normal will never be again.
Life will never be the same.
We have changed.
The world has shifted.
Soon we must ask
How then shall we live?

STONES
by Nadia Boulos

Hidden in the lush green,
Nestled in deep valleys,
Exposed on vast plains,
Ancient Stones bow to the rising sun
And glowing moon.

If only I were a stone on those structures,
I would trace back the history of a nation,
Document what people looked like
How they lived,
Art they created,
Plagues they endured,
Wars they wove,
Prayers, vows, hopes and dreams.

I would wave to them,
Then tell them
You are not alone,
Your pain, affliction, dying dreams
And rising hopes,
Are not singular.

I would reach out my arms
Through the limestone
And touch foreheads of little children,
Envelop their faces with my hands,
Hum a song of requiem,
Invite their souls into my bosom,
Caress them gently into sleep.

I would not question my existence
For I would know deep down
I was made to be leaned on
Stepped over
Pushed against
Climbed upon.

I would wipe away the blood and ichor
Splattered and shed all over my surface
I would instead raise the soil
Grow some green and maybe, just maybe
some color.

CROWD ENVY
by C.J. Prince

I cannot imagine
standing in line
at Fred Meyer,
nor venturing
to the dance floor
at the Wild Buffalo.

Will I ever lean in
to hear what you say?
How will the future
be safe?

How many COVID cycles
must run their course
to make
the next new world?

Who will we be now and then?
I waltz
the cat
around the kitchen.

WRITER IN QUARANTINE
by Mary Lou Haberman

Fifty-five days since last post,
settled into the Great Pause.

Frequent intention to write,
choosing instead to dance
with Distraction.

Needing less, feeling more.
Time morphs, then disappears.

Today is *Blursday*, right?

Juggling Grief's prism,
pleasures of piano.

New handle: *Boomer Zoomer*.

Walking the Interurban Trail
stunned by petals' shimmer.

Blessed with untarnished oxygen,
saddened by surge in freeway action.

THE COVID ENVELOPE
by JK Small

Within a lipid envelope lies
The genetic structure for coronavirus.

The envelope travels, takes flight, gains entry
By the simple act of taking a breath.

Invisible until it replicates repeatedly
In our lungs causing inflammation.

We've learned to do everything we can
To avoid the COVID envelope's delivery.

The envelope can be opened, its contents dissolved
Disintegrating with soap, water, and friction.

Our planet heals as we stay safe. The sky in Kathmandu
Now clear and blue, instead of hazy and gray.

Bees now pollinate apple blossoms in China
Birds migrate easily in skies without jet engines.

The highways are safer
As car accidents are on the decline.

No more mass shootings as classrooms are online
No more active shooters at concerts or at the mall.

Cyber life fills our days with Zoom meetings for work
For family gatherings and open mics.

We do curbside pick-ups, drive through testing
And have grown used to the sounds of delivery trucks.

We socialize from a distance, wear masks
While riding our bikes or walking on trails.

Windows open with sounds of music and applause
Banging pots and pans, and the beating of drums

While chanting from roof tops we honor
Our newfound celebrities of healthcare workers.

By the hundreds of thousands, death is pruning away
The old, debilitated, disenfranchised, and unlucky.

This has changed how we do business and communicate
How we work, shop, travel, teach and love.

For now, until a vaccine brings about herd immunity
We take temperatures, wash hands, cover our faces.

As we eat, pray, love in our bubble
Protecting ourselves and others from the COVID envelope.

LONGING
by Victoria Doerper

I long to make a quick trip to the store,
To linger in the produce section,
Fingering bumpy-skinned avocados
And the tender roundness of pears
Without fear of catching or transmitting
Anything except guacamole or cobbler.

I want to slip into a movie house,
Sit shoulder to shoulder with strangers
And listen to the hiss of their constant whispering
So I can feel benign annoyance
Instead of alarm
At someone not following the rules.
I want to share a tub of popcorn
With a friend, worrying only about
Whether there's too much butter.

I long to pet the dogs that cross my path
Without wondering about the health status
Of the person who last touched them;
I want to stand within smelling distance
Of anyone's aftershave or perfume.

I miss being awakened
By the roar and honking of trains
Between midnight and four a.m.,
And I pine for the silver curve of Amtrak
Sweeping into view, reliable as rain,
As I walk the shoreline in the morning.

I want to sit face-to-face with friends
Sharing wine and food and laughter.
I want to hug, long and hard,
Every single person I care about.
I want to go to church
And sing in my no-good-terrible voice
And know that someone sitting very near
Will have a beautiful voice louder than mine.

I want to think of the hospital
As a place of healing instead of harm,
To see doctors and nurses and helpers
As valued healers instead of victims of neglect.

I want to use my time well.
I want to try harder
To fix what is broken.
I long to be grateful for things
Before I lose them.

ON HAT CREEK
by Dick Little

If I stare at this campfire long enough,
Baking my moccasins while slivers
Of morning sunlight creep past my tent
And climb furrowed ponderosas
      That tower beside me;

While resolute boulders shoulder aside
Spring-full rapids rushing down the ages
Deafening the silence, will I heed
My bushy-tailed companion's advice
      From across Darwin's tree?

We watch each other, we two,
In glistening sunlight and wandering shadow,
Like Talmudic scholars, and chitter
On and on about existential mysteries
      Posed by a wiser God:

The space-time continuum,
Computer chips, viruses, espresso,
The square root of minus one—
Now, versus then. Or when.
      Or if.

UPON RECEIVING ADVICE OF A DOCTOR
by Joy Wright

To sit in it
Hear the news
Let it ruminate
In your mind
In your gut
In your heart
To wish to fight
But know you have little left
Save it for another day
A different battle
Let it wash over you like a tidal wave
Hold fast to your last straws
For those reeds will allow the oxygen in
Those will be the ropes that raise you up
Above the raging seas of despair.

QUESTIONS by Elizabeth Tervo

Is the lamp bright enough for you?
Is the heat turned up right for you?
I have questions.
You have answers.
But you won't tell them to me.
You keep them for yourself.

Are you wearing your coat?
Did you button up your coat?
You travel all around
and I stay here.
I'm afraid you might tell me a lie
just for some peace and quiet.

Where are we going? Is my black suit okay?
Will we be back by the end of the day?
If you look at me you'll see my hair is thinning
but you won't notice that if you sit down too.
Sit down too.
I know you have things to do.

When are you coming back to see me?
Will you come by plane, train, bus, boat, or taxi?
I don't mind sitting here alone
but I don't want to be left out.
I know well enough when I really will be left alone:
on the night my soul is required of me.

Did you put away your copy of my will?
Wait, wait for a minute, wait, while I take my pill.
I'm afraid you will forget me before then.
And so I throw out a question again.
Let's have a conversation, let's converse.
I still want to be part of your universe.

OH, TO BE A BIRD
by Penny Page

A bird can soar
And swirl and tip on the edge of air,
True freedom's flight
Above a lessening earth.

To watch the glide,
Humans tip their noses up
And dream the dream of wings.
But fate is sealed,
Their fate is done.
The try of old is squashed.

Envy strains
With wish and want to flee the pull of ground.
Limbs' pesky drag,
Anchor to uncertain being
Keep flow and languid single.

The bedlam runs and follows ground
And sighs as avians ascend away.

Oh, to be a bird.

BETWEEN THIS AND THAT
by Susan Chase-Foster

Somewhere,
Between a cry
And a scream
Is a realm
Of raw and rational
Vulnerability,
That feels as if
Your heart
Has been ripped out
By its roots
From your chest.

This is called fear.

Somewhere,
Between a sigh
And a dream
Is a vague sense
Of possibilities
Diminished,
That feels as if
You've missed
A turn on a trail
You never meant
To set out on.

This is called lost.

Somewhere,
Between your eye
And your spleen
Is a pair of lungs,
Your holy bellows
Of aspiration,
Divine air balloons
Filling and emptying,
That feels as if
The invisible Mouth of God
Is playing you like a flute.

This is called alive.

A SILVER LINING by Susan Greisen

When I trained as a nurse at age nineteen, I had one goal:
to serve and help those in need.
I didn't expect a fat paycheck,
great adoration, or an annual bonus.
It was never about any of those selfish desires.

For my fifty years in the healthcare industry,
my employers gave me three items of gratitude:
a cake knife,
a monogrammed coffee mug,
and a lapel pin designating my years of service.

If I were lucky enough to work on
Thanksgiving or Christmas,
I received a turkey dinner in the hospital cafeteria.
An HMO honored me at an anniversary banquet.
None of us expected more than that.

Then one day COVID-19 landed on the world's doorstep.
Media information barraged our minds.
Millions of patients were infected,
thousands died,
including frontline workers.

Over 11% of America's frontline staff were infected,
many died including janitors, counselors, social workers,
respiratory therapists, dietary staff, doctors, nurses.
The images and statistics were devastating.
COVID-19 holds no bounds.

Soldiers have an expectation of military battles.
War games help them prepare.
In modern times only a few healthcare workers experienced
the pandemic/epidemic abyss of Ebola, HIV, MERS, or SARS.
COVID-19 is another beast.

Managing pandemics was never an expectation
of today's healthcare workers.
Yes, we performed disaster drills.
Mannequins, actors, and fake blood tested our skills.
But no one was prepared for COVID-19.

As I stood in my protective bubble—six feet apart and masked,
I recently met two new neighbors.
One shared the story of her husband's chronic illness.
My questions to her indicated my interest
as a retired nurse.

Their eyes lit up when I said the word
"nurse."
Not knowing me or my work history
the other neighbor said, "Thank you for your service."
My heart swelled by her appreciation.

I've received many thanks from my patients and their families,
but never a thank you from a complete stranger.
Unsolicited gratitude, special discounts, and parking spaces
seem only reserved for veterans of war,
not for healthcare workers.

Maybe a silver lining has been found
in this new kind of war—COVID-19.
The world's unsung healthcare heroes were thrust into the
limelight.
Nothing, absolutely nothing, is more precious than life.
Yes, freedom *is* important and worth fighting for.

But if you do not have
life,
you cannot enjoy
freedom.

2020 CD3 + CO VI
by Nancy Canyon

My car is not cut out to be a moon, though it gets
me from here to there and the mileage is not bad.
However, the back is cluttered with candy wrappers,
soiled masks, articles of clothing, and my grandson's
forgotten schoolwork dated March 15th. Up front, the
mats are littered with gum wrappers, toothpicks, gas
receipts, and empty sanitizer bottles. If my car were
a moon, it would chug past in the night—Pig Pen's
dust trailing comet-like behind. My car is not a moon,
but a Woody Wagon-sized comet orbits the earth every
47 days, and it is in pristine shape, just like when
first marketed in 1949. Now that seems moon worthy.

PRESCRIPTION FOR A SHELTERING IN PLACE DAY by Joe Nolting

Pull off the mask
put the gloves aside
open the window wide

listen to the pulse
of raindrops against
the fresh earth

hear the juncos'
call and response
the soft echo of desire

inhale the sweet scent
of cottonwood leaves
breathe in so deeply

you dislodge the sorrow
that has taken residence
near your heart

witness the swallow
knife its way through the air
as if it could tear open

the morning's fragile fabric
and your burdens could
leak through the fissure

imagine the day now
changed, the earth tilting
gently away from pain.

GETTING BY
by Carol McMillan

I shop mostly at the
Kamuela farmers' markets now:
Eggs, bananas, macadamia nuts,
Vanilla, lilikoi jelly...
Add a few tablespoons of flour:
Banana nut pancakes!
Drizzle with Amaretto.

SUCH A LITTLE THING
by Brenda M. Asterino

Such a little thing.
It stirred our focus
More in three months
Than in fifty years.

In so little time,
A virus stopped
And flipped our lives,
Knocking us breathless.

Did we dream it?
This bug-eyed nightmare,
An unseen thug
On body and mind?

'Til it wrought through heart
A fever from our souls,
For equality
In our nation.

PREPARATIONS FOR A HUG
by Cami Ostman

Don freshly laundered clothing
Wash your hands
And face
And hair
But not more than twenty minutes
Before the intended hug.

Inquire as to the quarantine habits
Of your prospective co-hugger.

Has there been other
human contact
in the last fourteen days?

This conversation should
happen over the phone.

Meet one another outside
In the sunshine
And hope there is no breeze.
Wind propels droplets
Of mucus through the air
And we do not want to be caught
In one another's slipstream

Stand six feet apart
Open arms
Your face should be directed to the left
Your partner should do the same
As if in a mirror
Away from you
Move forward quickly
Embrace

Hold for Three. Two. One.
Dislodge.
And quickly sanitize yourself
with a grapefruit scented
rubbing alcohol spritz.

ARK by Joe Nolting

The pandemic's rising
floodwaters seep
into the nursing home

where my father,
like so many of his tribe
has been held hostage.

Today I'll break down
the door, rip it into
a million wood splinters

stitch them together
piece-by-piece
build a boat

cubit-by-cubit
bigger than Noah's memory
I'll lay down the gangplank

watch the nursing home tribe
approach like scared animals
nervously sniff the air

test the steepness
of the climb ahead
then, slowly, two-by-two

walkers and wheelchairs
they will rise above
the floodwaters of their fear

shuffle onto the Ark
walkers and wheelchairs
crowding the deck.

THE SLIME OF SLUGS
by Carol McMillan

COVID-19 moves like a corpulent slug,
Depositing eggs along an invisible slime trail.
Odorless and colorless, the slug slides among us,
Leaving no detectable evidence of its passage.
I wish we could see its fuchsia scent,
Taste its slimy tolling,
Or touch its loathsome flavor,
Anything to warn us of its presence.
Too late, we do respond,
We do detect its trail,
But not until it has its way with us:
Cancelling a graduation,
postponing a tennis tournament,
And eliminating our jobs.
A million eggs have hatched,
A million offspring
Gunging their way across Planet Earth.
With the barest trace of their ooze
They are felling playwrights, actors, political figures,
And your best friend's grandma.
We curse the slugs
And watch them shrivel beneath the salt of tears
Shed in their murderous wake.
Tender as newborns,
We thread our lives together,
Newly awakened to the web of life necessary
To sustain us all.

HANDS 1 by BeDo

In medical school, she marveled
Tissues and tendons cast to articulate a smile
Form words from thin air. The face, a landscape
Of untold beauty. And then
Tasked to dissect
A human hand
She wept. Unfurling five fingers
A universe appeared
History itself

These days, I pause in moments untangling
Hair strands swept across my temples
Circling soap round and round
Blue cup rims, watch how
Note by note, a symphony of movement plays
Simple as weather
Awestruck by each exquisite miracle my fingers
Willingly do

Pressed in prayer, palm to palm
Such as pilgrims the bard once penned
I now hold my own hand
In ways few men ever cared to learn

This uncommon solitude has become a gentle lacing
Deep longing with nature's grace
A moment in history when mine, like lovers'
Lucky to fumble, are as blessed
As stoic old couples'
Reaching through the clouds
Or across the table
To hold on
To whatever remains
After this storm

ESSENTIAL WORKERS
by Gary Wade

do, repeat
do, repeat
fast work
hard work
dangerous
exhausting
under-paid

do, repeat
do, repeat
do, repeat
tiring

distraction
Corona
accidents
maim or kill
   disposable
human capital
of capitalism
do, repeat
do, repeat

HELPLESSNESS
by Rebecca Mabanglo-Mayor

Stark
white linoleum
bounced the pings
and buzzes from
dozens of
monitors
along
the emergency
wing where he
stood waiting, waiting
waiting for
word
about
not one
but two loved
ones struck down
in one
afternoon.
why.

MORNING TURN-AROUND
by Gary Wade

Someone lodged a door or two
south of the carriage house
is clattering her piano—
an old, upright birdcage from the trang of it—
playing Maple Leaf Rag.

Her skill is maybe not the best,
a few notes bent or left astray,
but she has so polished up this morning
that started out so dismal despite
the morning sun's triumphant amber glow.

She segued onward into other rags
that I cannot name, and I don't know hers.
I hope she'll play more often
with windows open to day and air;
let me know her only by her hands.

I'll sit among the garden iris,
—listen—
and watch the new-day tulips grow
flaming to music
in morning's golden light.

PURPOSE by Joe Nolting

A disembodied voice
drifts over the grocery store
intercom like a lost dream
snakes its way down aisle ten

where the young woman kneels
on the unforgiving tile floor
sweeps a lock of brilliant
pink hair from her forehead

tightens the paper mask
covering her nose and mouth
stacks cans on the empty shelf
fills in the dark, hungry space

creates a perfect cube of
black beans, chicken broth
beef stew, tomato soup
each can a brick shoring up

the foundation of sustenance
a bulwark of comfort
against scarcity and fear's
insatiable appetite

The young woman peers at
the embossed tag on her lapel
sees she is no longer Pam
or Nancy or Susan

but has a new identity
a name solid like the steel can
she stacks so carefully
heavy with the weight of purpose.

THE ESSENCE
by Carol McMillan

Today
Existence
Shrinks and swells,
Looming or squeaking by,
Depending on the mood.

Existence
Fills each cycle
As the sun and moon
Chase each other around the planet.

The illusions of reasons for being
Have been felled by a virus.
The screens through which
We have viewed our lives
Are wiped clean,
Undifferentiated by those
Illusory deadlines
We've held dear.

There remains only
Essential existence
For our contemplation.

BREATHE FIRST
by Isabel Castro

Through breath, this stealthy virus weaves through our
communities.

She challenges us to breathe slowly and steadily, *in situ*.
What if we were to breathe first, before falling to her tight
grip?

What if we slowed down,
inhaling deeply,
exhaling fully,
and reconnected with our own inner rhythms?

She guides us each back home—within our walls, within our
bodies.
*"Let go of unreasonable expectations. Cherish what you have.
Clean your home, but also your mind, actions, and community."*

What can I shed?
What would I do with extra time?
How do I support my community?
What are my priorities, and do I nurture them?

Somehow I'd forgotten to care about the essentials.

She primed us to see
our brother underfoot
air squeezed out
his mama running for him from the other side.

How many breaths have I taken for granted,
while my brothers, sisters, and cousins had theirs stripped
away?

As eyes open, blood pulses, heart breaks, and mind races,
How can I keep a steady breath?

As masks of hatred and compliance fall,
Faces still covered with virus protection,
We are ready, willing, and already weary for a long road ahead,
with a list of new essentials for us all.

Somehow she feels like mama,
helping us from the other side,
to breathe slowly and steadily, *in situ*.

THE Cs
by Abbe Rolnick

I see you
Even if you hide
I feel the despair
Of illness

The world suffers
A pandemic virus
Uncovered
Before our eyes

Unfair you say
Know my pains
I plead in dismay
See me

Cancer lives inside me
And I endure
No pity
But see me

For I am you
Human in this race
Humbled
Be the grace

LOOK WITH YOUR EYES
by Laura Rink

Look with your eyes, not your hands
my mother said in gift shops, antique stores, museums.

Now, in my mask and gloves, I peer at
avocados and apples, grapefruit and lemons

using my eyes to discern
firmness, ripeness, compatibility

wondering if the underside of the apple holds a bruise,
if the grapefruit will be more rind than flesh.

Touching is a commitment—
you are now mine, for better or for worse.

CANDLES AND CRADLES
by Betty Scott

in loving memory of Lily Copelan

A bout with COVID-chaos rocks us now,
and once again there is a quickening,
a call of emotions that sets our eyes

blinking and roving. Married, as we are,
to social constructions of wealth and poverty,
beneath veils of conflicting desires,

we're called once again to question
identities, displacements, reasons
to exist, encouraged within

the breath-taking fury and fog of grief
to think of our self as a stock,
merged to buy each other out.

No wonder, poets who struggle to speak,
each word exact and in right order,
learn, soon enough, about settlements,

about bodies as cellular prisons and gifts,
since, poets too, send Giant Redwoods
and Douglas Firs to the saws.

These days of predictions
and dire fruitions,
species flickering out,

why not waken from dormancy,
desires as humble as
stanzas and phrases,

candles and cradles,
cords of light to whisper,
rock, and nurture love?

Why not bow and vow,
for sprouts' sake,
to title each song "Obsession?"

CONCATENATION
by Susan Chase-Foster

As I sprinkle salt
Over a casserole
Of sweet potatoes
Perfumed with curry,
A hazelnut-clutching
Squirrel stops running
Across our neighbor's roof,
Looks down at me as if
He knows something I don't.
An egg-bulboused spider
Swings from a bamboo branch
To our kitchen window,
Taps "Be safe!" on the glass
With all eight legs.
A masked man worries
His way through an arroyo
He's felt safe walking on
For twenty years.
An elderwoman shuffles
To the sliding glass doors
Of her townhouse, gazes
Out at the whitecapped
Salish Sea, gasps with
Overwhelming gratitude
For rain, for clouds, for breath,
For one more day.
A baby is born.
Someone dies, another dies.
Someone takes a breath
For the first time
Unchained to a ventilator.
A poet is unable to write

Even a single word,
Another nearly drowns
In the flood of pandemic images
Pouring through her pen.
I slip a casserole
Of sweet potatoes
Perfumed with curry,
A sprinkle of salt,
And a cupful of moments
Linked by an invisible virus
Into the oven.

LOSING OUR ELDERS
by Kate Miller

Listen, we are losing our Elders
by the week, by the day, by the hour.
They are slipping away from us
before we have time to miss them.

Everywhere they are dying alone
in their homes, in hospital hallways,
in line to be tested, to be admitted,
to be accepted or rejected, to be seen.

We cannot be with them as they die.
Cannot hug them, cannot carry them,
cannot hold them close or whisper
in their ear, cannot say our goodbyes.

We cannot bury our elders, cannot gather
together to honor them, praise them,
tell our stories of them, remember them.
We cannot complete the circle of our grief.

TRIPTYCH
by Laura Rink

History, Repeating
In 1918, my Armenian grandmother
remained in a village in Turkey
while the Spanish flu made a pilgrimage
through the genocide-infected desert.

In 2020, her granddaughter
remained at home in America
while COVID-19 continued its stealth mission
through the inequitable country.

Freedom
In 1975, my Armenian grandmother, now
a proud American citizen, wrote:

A true freedom can only be attained
through responsibility and respect.

Responsibility—own your role in a racist society.
Respect—listen, with your ears, not your mouth.

Responsibility—wear a mask.
Respect—stay six feet away.

History, Making
Virus propagates, prejudice seeps.
A vaccine, perhaps,
yet no such inoculation for bigotry.

You remain a host
for a disease that has outlived
every genocide and pandemic to date.

HARMONY
by Rebecca Mabanglo-Mayor

Cooperation
begins with
knowing our survival
is assured when
resources are
shared,
freely
when we
look at each
other without fear,
prejudice or
animosity.

DAY 53
by Shannon Laws

If the world were normal now,
as it may never be again,
I might enjoy the morning.
This morning where I woke,
at 8:37 a.m., ate breakfast
drank coffee in bed, started writing,
and still under the sheets at 11:36.

If this was, let's say, Friday, September 20, 2019,
I would not label this morning a case of *pandemic fatigue*,
no—it would be *relaxation*.

It is what the pre-pandemic modern world
used to refer as a "personal day."
(remember personal days?)
I could find joy in working at home if all
my neighbors got into their cars and
drove to work this morning!
THEN today would be a special day for me.
But, it is not.

It is day 53 of the lockdown, and there is nothing
but the heavy responsibility of
staying home and
saving lives.

ON STONE
by Gary Wade

Stone has no soul
but ofttimes there is
a certain hardness of spirit.

I love and respect
water stones,
they hold stories,
are well-rounded.

Wind stones are eccentric
but they stand tall,
still
secret histories exposed.

Stone is known for silence
but it has a talent
for throwing echoes.

THE SUMMER OF THE PLAGUE: 1665
by Laura Kalpakian

Heat ripples off the bricks in this walled and windless English garden. Satiated stillness. Nothing moves or has moved. No breath of a breeze. The frog, the fly, the ladybugs, even they are stationary, listless, lethargic as is the ungainly young man sprawled upon the summer grass. Safe from the plague ravaging Europe, Isaac Newton lies on his back. Sleep tempts him, flirts with him as does sunlight fringing the unruffled leaves above him.

They seem larger, greener, beaded with humidity, gleaming optically as light and time pass obliquely through the branches overhead. Suddenly, breaking the silence, breaking the stillness, a stem audibly attenuates. Snaps. An object plummets to earth, drops, plops, bounces, rolls, and comes to rest beside Isaac.

(And he is Isaac, a young man. Not yet Sir Isaac Newton. Not yet hyphenated and enclosed, walled within [1642-1727] not yet marmoreally entombed in Westminster Abbey, not yet entombed in textbooks, for that matter, where his laws are numbered, and his gravity beyond question until the wiry-white-haired Einstein spoke relatively of space and time, and light and energy, opened nature to the universe, or maybe vice versa, before Einstein, too, was walled and hyphenated, enclosed within [1879-1955].)

Curious, Isaac rolls over, pondering the under-ripe apple that lies motionless until two ladybugs land on it, nod to one another, and wink at him. Nearby, a self-satisfied frog smiles his wide-slit smile. His belly billows out, his tongue flashes, snatches one ladybug from the apple (that rolls on its stemless axis, motion, mass and energy transformed). The frog hops away. The remaining ladybug flies away. The young man looks aloft, recreates the apple's trajectory, imagines its cosmic course. *Aha!* Revelation!

Revelation! Inspiration! Bring Isaac quickly to his feet, breaking up his state of rest, as he is compelled to motion, away from the shade, the walled garden, the grass, sprinting toward the library, his desk, the quill-and-ink with which he will commit his *Aha!* to paper, *Philosophiae Naturalis Principia Mathematica,* 1687, a work edited and financed by Edmond Halley who himself became a comet.

Sir Isaac will always ponder that infinitesimal sliver of time. What if he had slept and missed the apple? He believes the ladybugs did indeed wink at him, nod, collude, connive to convince and inspire *Aha!* Revelation! He will resent them, yes, and that fat-bellied frog too. Where were they when Sir Isaac really needed inspiration, revelation? And where was the apple for that matter? When for the next sixty years a great fruitless quest absorbed his life and mind. He will be knighted, and yet forever benighted, totally stumped in his search for the alchemist's secret: how to turn lead into gold. He will die unrequited.

Nonetheless, for centuries Newton's portrait hangs in over-warm classrooms. *Newton's law states that motion has laws and stillness does not* drones the teacher as the students slump, and gravity pulls their heads down down down because revelation, once codified into Law, printed in leather bound volumes with all due gravity, loses all *Aha!* As the teacher well knows. Still, he continues, *Every body continues in its state of rest or uniform motion unless it is compelled to change...*

Every body? Everybody? The living and the dead? The hale and farewell? Every body cut from the whole cloth of humanity, from memory that tatters, pales, and fades with light and time? Light bends when it passes obliquely from one medium to another. We call this refraction. Time bends when it passes obliquely from one medium to another. We call this diffusion. We all diffuse and refract, endlessly so, subject to laws we never agreed to, save in becoming flesh, and thus susceptible to death, to grief, to hunger, lust, and summertime.

STILL
by Kate Miller

Each morning now there's a new pause
between sleep and waking, a jolt where
we remember, again, that our world is
no longer what it was before. We try to
turn away, curl back into familiar warmth,
pull covers over our heads, now we are
awake, our routine tinted by trepidation.

Still the sun rises.

Every day we gather at the table,
drinking our morning tea, reading
news. In our sunny kitchen the day
seems so reasonable, rational and
calm, there is no urgency, no place
we need to go, while all the while a
scream is building in my chest.

And still the sun rises.

This morning, my guard down, I read
every day more jobs lost, overwhelmed
food banks, over 800 people waiting, lines
snake down roads, people everywhere
need what help they can find. I feel tears
spill out, prelude to the scream's escape.
Swallow hard, force it back down.

And still the moon rises.

Now the scream's pushing back again,
gathering behind heart's door. Not
wanting to be silenced it grows, feeds
on fears of scarce ventilators, defective
masks, all hospitals full of exhaustion
and despair. Its backbeat is the rising
wail of every late night ambulance.

And still the moon rises.

Soon it will bust its way up my throat,
sliding past clenched teeth, enter the
world in a roar, joining other screams,
burning through all the separation,
isolation, one collective scream, prey
stalked by predators that just might
turn out to be of our own making.

Still the moon rises.

HANDS II by BeDo

I watch couples sailing past my gate
Morning, noon, night. Fingers

Safely harbored inside slips
Small affectionate vessels, touching

Interlaced lives
Relationships

I wake to a vision
Homes are ablaze, sparks

Heat
All the ingredients of explosion

Fire has a temper
As does change

Birds strip cones from nearby trees
Drop them into the inferno

Meanwhile, their fledglings, mouths gaping
Soar into the sky

Today
Something must burn

Tomorrow
Something must open

Water cups in palms pressed together
Races between fingers outstretched

Wings and seeds
Wings and seeds

TILTING WORLD
by Brenda M. Asterino

Shifting sand, our world quakes,
As global shrinks and drifts.
Dis-ease storm shakes us all
As time fails to inform.

Lonely burns. We're letting go,
To find some peace inside.
Our countenance towards others
Proves nobler strength abides.

Food banks use six feet of space
To lift up hope and cope.
We boldly go to zooming;
Communing, "or be damned."

Frayed reflections while on hold,
We stand to light the way!
Hues of life are crystalline;
And hold our fears at bay.
Even with face covered
Silent signals grace and play.

Charting cost in culture change,
No life can be lost.
Spit and dirt across our souls
Wash away our blindness.
Our compass is Community.
The Architect is Kindness.

LESS REFINED
by Jean Waight

Some days I live
In a bottomless mug.

Ritually we change
Tea to coffee
And back to tea again
In the afternoons.
News is endless,
I'm braless,
Listless,
Witless.

Other days I rouse
Shower and spiff.
List.
Venture out.
The town is new,
Somehow younger.
Mount Bakery the place
For treats, but now
They bake bread,
The staff of life
In a scratchy
Whole grain style
I've longed for.

I regain my wits.
The times I knew
Aren't coming back,
But I'm back.
Less refined.
More determined.

SOCIAL DISTANCING
by Joe Nolting

I have mastered the mathematics
of social distancing, memorized
only one true measurement

six feet, my height, two full paces
the length of a sofa, width of a car
a soaring eagle's wingspan

six feet, our new standard of safety
the gap separating you from me
as if we were lonely castles

surrounded by freshly dug moats
but today the only hole we dig
is for the newly fallen, a fresh grave

six feet down in the dark earth
my exact height, two full paces
the distance you stand from me

at the edge, as we peer down
calculate the fragile journey
the wingspan of an eagle.

LOSERS AND WINNERS OF COVID-19
by Susan E. Greisen

Losers: The economy
Winners: The environment

Losers: Shuttered small businesses
Winners: Take out, home delivery, curbside made ends meet

Losers: People with comorbidities
Winners: Those who left the hospital after weeks in ICU

Losers: Elderly living alone
Winners: Neighbors and friends helping isolated seniors

Losers: Narrow-mindedness and unsubstantiated opinions
Winners: Science and metrics

Losers: Extroverts
Winners: Introverts

Losers: Extroverts again
Winners: Reincarnated extroverts writing poetry

Losers: Cancelled vacation plans
Winners: Rediscovering your own backyard, your community

Losers pre-COVID: The drudgery of grocery shopping
Winners during COVID-19: Any excuse to leave the house

Losers pre-COVID: Dreading vaccinations
Winners during COVID-19: Hope for a vaccine

Losers: The disgust of wearing a mask
Winners post-COVID-19: The day we will no longer need one

HOW TO BE ALONE
by Nancy Canyon

Pretend you are not alone. Write out a fake schedule; one that is overly busy. Decide you cannot possibly get everything done and cancel all dates. Start with driving your mother-in-law to the dentist in Seattle. Suggest a local dentist. Tell your neighbor, *So sorry, I cannot water your lawn today. Isn't it supposed to rain tonight?* Canceled! Your schedule is now clear; you feel refreshed, almost like standing beside the pond, reaching hands toward blue sky above. Really, being alone is akin to flying a glider, silent and empty, far above the earth, free at last.

PANDEMIC PROCRASTINATION
by Dick Little

(Covidus Interruptus)

So, where *is* that manuscript?
(Scrolling the screen.) Such a great story.
Ten years in. Perfect time to finish it.
What was that title? It's in my "Writing" file
　　　　somewhere.

Next to "Photos." (What great pics.
Dang, that was a great vacation!
France. And then the summer cabin in Glacier.
Wait? Whose adorable kittens are those?)

I have *got* to email my cousin,
The one in Montana—not young anymore—
Just to check on how he's doing,
COVID-19 and all. But first, get to work here.

Work! Wow, what if this had hit before I retired?
Work from home? Laid off? Fired!
Like all those folks strolling our street.
Who knew there were so many
　　　　breeds of dog!

Whew, found the MSS. How's this for
　　　　a title?
"It's A Wonderful Life."
(Global Disease Spoiler Alert.)
Okay, may need to change that

But hey, this reads pretty good.
"The days stretched out ahead
Like a fabulous picnic, spread on a checkered blanket..."

Oh crap! What's for dinner? Cooking in again.
Pick-up meals don't travel well.
Burgers don't sizzle. Fries, lukewarm.
Don't even start about pancakes and over-easy eggs
From my fav breakfast place.

Even if dining at restaurants is now okay,
No way I'm ready for that, swapping invisible viri aerosol
With who-knows which diner hasn't distanced.
Plus, elastic on the face mask makes my ears stick out,
            like Dopey.

"...[O]n a checkered blanket." Okay, can't lead with food,
Or happy days ahead. Hmm, "days ahead like empty streets."
Then, tone down the optimism, but not too dreary.
S**t, I'm *not* going to rewrite the whole damn thing.

Looks pretty complete now, actually: beginning, middle, end.
Hook, arc, and all. Is ten thousand words too short for a
novella?
Gotta know when to stop, right?
I mean I don't have a lot of time for a full do-over.

Oh. Yeah.
Just the rest of my life.

ONCE UPON THE EARTH by BeDo

We were falling at an unprecedented rate
Limbs weak, our families ripped apart
Someone, please ~
Temperatures rising, burning fevers
Inside our eldest, every cell gasped
Wave upon wave, death, destruction
Too much, too many, someone please
Go ~
As they continued to bulldoze our grandmothers
Into the ground, so many unnatural departures
Fish jumped out of water. A signal.
Please, hurry! Go ~
As they threw us in crates, disposed of our bodies
Used our blood, scientific experiments
Bird's eye caught the sign. Flew for days
Whispered to Moth
You are of the night. You must go ~
As they fought amongst themselves, toppling
Monuments, making rules, deaf to anything
But their own desires, their own needs
Moth fluttered through the darkness
Her wings ached. Even so, she pressed on
Bird had not consumed her
Had not taken her life; the message, our message
Thrummed inside her
This is a matter of Life or Death! Go ~
From tree to tree, over river and mountain
Moth flew
So tired now
Still she was going
So frail now
She had to keep going
Almost extinct now
She couldn't give up!

She was going to Bat
For us
All.

PRAYER
by Brenda M. Asterino

If Prayer was made to bind us in faith
Then have we not found treasure
As sisters and brothers stand with one another?

If Prayer is irresistible force
Then we best never forget
This transformative path that jelled community.

If Prayer was made to unify us
Then I want to remember
When COVID became the immovable object.

If Prayer was made for reflection.
Then were we not given the time
For all minds to see reality in the USA?

If Prayer was made to change perspective
Then were not petitions answered
As our hearts heard the
Call for all and
Larger love became wider action?

As Prayer transmutes fear to feeling strong
Then are we the solution?
Is this a true revolution
As we decide to achieve one humanity?

May this Prayer be an action.
May we experience real change.
May voices, hearts, and hands
Be a triumph of justice.

AS USUAL
by Mary Lou Haberman

Four fat chickens cluck in the front yard.
As usual.

A handsome young man
in faded jeans, beard, Birkenstocks,
stops while his ebony dog
sniffs the hens.

The dog bounces,
snout poking
through chicken wire,
eager to come nose to beak
with the confident birds.
As usual.

I greet the man,
we lower our masks.
Once our glasses defog, we lock eyes!
Oh, the relief.
I delight in his calm
face full with dimples and smile.

Yet, I feel slimy, mucked up, contagious.
We keep the distance.
No more usual.

Your dog is gorgeous, I say.
I want to pet him.
I can't.
Used to.
No more usual.

Thanks, his name is Socrates.
Just got him as a rescue.

I want us to be rescued.
We are blanketed by the Great Pause.
Innocent. Captive.
I want us to be rescued immediately.

I miss the usual.

We talk about the invasion.
The virus. The invisible enemy.
The silent scourge that has no life
yet sucks life and livelihood
from so many around the world.
We mention the victims, the changes.
The unknown future.

We admit
the future
has always been unknown.

But this time it's different.

As usual,
I ask, how is your family?

Kenya only has a few cases.
They're careful.
They're OK so far.

We know the new meaning of *so far*.

But my wife has been sick.

I freeze.
Embarrassed
to find myself backing away.
Does he sense my retreat?

As usual, I say sorry to hear that.

Thanks.
He shrugs
and shakes his head
as if to reassure me.

I collect myself.
How is she?

Oh she's fine now.
Feels good.
Working from home.

Oh good, I say from the distance.
Further away than usual.

We talk again about the chickens.
Socrates is satisfied with his adventure.

The man and I remask,
taking a long moment
to be sure we are safe
for each other,
from each other.

There is the usual goodbye,
have a great day.

Then we take turns
blessing each other.

Be safe.
The newly required mantra.

He walks on with Socrates.
I turn back.
The chickens cluck
as I weep.

LESSON FROM A ROBIN
by Victoria Doerper

My teacher today
Is not online.
She lingers outside
Scarlet-breasted,
Bold-eyed,
Wearing feathers.
No teacher I ever had
Dared dress and act
Like that,
As if she were auditioning
For some risqué
Broadway musical.
I'm sitting on the porch
In my pajamas,
Reading the news
And feeling so sad,
Ignoring everything around me.
Ms. Robin chirps, dips, and hops.
Repeatedly. Then swoops
In a long arc in front of me.
If she had a ruler
She'd rap my hands.
Look, she says,
Pay very close attention.
Here's today's lesson.
Even you
Should be able to understand.
I'm rummaging in the dirt,
Dodging your neighbor's cat,
Thrilled to be eating worms.
And I'm damn well singing.

HAVE I TOLD YOU
by C.J. Prince

This day, the turning day,
just another pandemic day,
but a day of shift on faerie wings.

This day, I do not remember
what I have said, if I told
or assumed you knew—

Did I forget, or did you?
On this day when anything
can happen, gilded or gutted,

whether we forgot to dance
and wear ribbons in our hair,
it is an allotted time

of togetherness
in our own shelters,
you there, me here.

This day, all days,
rain and new rose leaves,
like all days,

I can write the possible
or impossible.
But this day I tell you

I love you. You,
just as you are,
just this moment

suppressing terror,
knowing flaws and flairs,
not knowing you at all.

This day, I love you,
wherever you are,
I cannot see,

nor you me,
behind my black
mask and low brim hat.

But now we have walked
the edge of oblivion
together,

and for each day that follows,
in all cross quarter days,
remember, I love you.

MEAT-BEE
by Elizabeth Tervo

All summer we've been in our prime
Searching and finding, nectar and pollen,
Husbands and wives.
We spent hours exploring the flowers
hours that lasted like centuries.

Then, one green tree sported one yellow leaf.
The white of a birch shone out.
One dry leaf fell. The sky is that extra blue
that comes when the heat goes.
Sailing clouds take center stage.

The sunlight slants different.
We don't know how we know it
but we know that we are moving toward our end.
Let's get our claws into one last ferocious meal.

EXISTENTIALISM IN THE TIME OF COVID
by BeDo

That thing came in again
You know, as the saying goes
When you least expect it
It showed up—as echo, a clanging bell
On a buoy bobbing out there somewhere
In the sea of *what if* and *who cares anyway*
Where barges of memory and future thoughts
Float their massive cargos to and fro

What does it matter, these words
For whom? Why? What good do they do?
What's good? Who cares? Why care?
Rather stare at tree bark all day, watch how
It breathes like a festooned hummingbird breast
But much much slower and not quite as bright

Yesterday, I wrote a story in my head
The kind where people cry at the last page
Then throw it in the fire
Because it's all wood words, and both burn
Hot and unanswered

Why is a question for god and children
Who know the response is just another question
So, instead of asking, study
How the red ant circles back halfway around
The limb, finds its way home
By sensing where others in its colony
have come from
How quietly, on the horizon, ships meet
Somewhere around sunset
To exchange yesterday for
Tomorrow

CORONA CROWN OF CONS
by Abbe Rolnick

Confusion reigns as COVID-19 spreads
Invisible as it travels uncontained
Contagious in the hearts and lungs
Of those we love
Contagious in the loss of income
Confusion reigns as presidential mandates
Contradict health experts
Contagious anxiety transforms
Us to introverts
Silenced into isolation
Confusion reigns until our soul
Rises to inspiration
Contagious needs to control
Spawns art, song, dance
Confined to six feet of social distance
Confusion reigns with inconsistent rules
Crazed illogical decisions
Forces more divisions
Contagious spread of conspiracies
Misaligned information
Filters sift for consolation
Confusion reigns as elders die
Children question why
Crave hugs and kisses
Everyone misses
Confusion reigns till vaccinations
Reach across the world
In ceremonious coronations.

SHADOWS OF THE MADRONE
by Jennifer Mueller

Summer teases glistening waves out the window
while the madrone stands in silent watch
weaving through the air in lime green and rust red

An orca surfaces breaking the calm
with shouts of welcome
"Look before it is gone!" And then summer is.
The summer that never was.

Mist rolls in off the water blanketing the land in grey
papery red curls litter the damp ground
beneath twisted skeletal arms of the madrone

bleached white branches
breaking through the living
moss slowly covers with the return of dripping skies

Perfect white flowers in spring
the scent of the forest bright in the air
brilliant berries in fall, a raven settles from flight

None of that is seen now out the window
As we huddle inside while the world pauses
sinuous shadows spreading, curving, twisting, reaching
while seals pop their heads up
beneath the madrone

NORMAL
by Lisa Dailey

January 2020 held promise of a new year
As the WHO declared a global health emergency.
I'm oblivious to the outside world.

In February COVID-19 is officially named
And making its way to my state.
I'm finalizing spring and summer travel plans.

By March the words coronavirus and pandemic
Fight to attract my attention.
Nightly news becomes my new habit.

Italy in chaos, then France, then the UK
Travel from Europe to the US is banned.
Sleep disruption is my new routine.

School cancelled, then prom, then graduation
Every trip I've planned is postponed.
I long for a return to normal.

Countries are locked down, Olympics delayed,
The US leads the world in confirmed cases.
I can't comprehend 100,000 dead.

A million sick by April, millions more unemployed,
Countries plunge to recession, world leaders hospitalized.
Can we ever get back to normal?

Our president peddles snake oil and emboldens protest
While armed white men scream at police.
I know if the men were Black, they'd be dead.

A light in these times, the environment rebounds
As the world ceases to abuse it.
Maybe normal isn't the ideal I should aim for.

In May the world watches George Floyd
Killed by police, sparking a new national eruption
I can't breathe.

My country fights wars on two fronts
Many challenge systemic racism, but not near enough
I have much to learn.

2020 no longer holds promise.
We must learn from our mistakes,
Make better choices,

Fight for those in need, elect those who can lead
Educate ourselves, wear a fucking mask.
Normal will never be ok again.

THANK YOU
by Brenda M. Asterino

Thank you to the people,
The masses of the nation.
Thank you to the foreign hearts
Who gave us prayers and gifts
Of masks, PPEs,
And ventilators.

Thank you to the worker-bees;
Nurses, aides, doctors, therapists,
Tool makers, seamstresses, and 3D nerds.
Drivers, repair people, food workers, electricians,
Architects, modular inventors, tent owners,
All volunteers everywhere,
Firemen, EMS, and police giving aid,
And all I don't remember.

These are the powerless who protect and care.
They give everything they have...
Every last drop
Of internal strength.
And then,
They give their own safety.

Thanks to those with a friendly smile
For the people who lost
All three of their jobs.
For making them feel
A part of the larger culture
Enough
To ask for help.

If you've given that smile, that work,
That everything,
Thank you.

Last but not least,
Thank you to parents
Who spend sleepless nights
On how to keep their children safe.
Who keep going
When everything is gone.
Who stay, stand, and fight
For their children
So tomorrow
Will be better.

Thank you
To those who give a little
And to those who give everything,
And to those who gave the ultimate,
You are the midwives of Humanity.

REESTABLISHING TRUST
by Joy Wright

As our country reopens
we move closer together
first with close neighbors
and friends as businesses open
we go back to work
back to the parks
and shopping
lower our face masks
begin to live
more like it used to be
and numbers soar
and we freeze
like red light green light
in a backyard
we don't want to be caught
we don't want to be 'it'
so we stand frozen like a statue
until green light or the next phase
is called again.

DUST TO DUST
by Nancy Canyon

~On a line from David Yezzi

Some ancient stories begin with a sickness—
I have no line, no answer, no prediction, yet
I do know more will die. How I worry that
coronavirus will be like the Spanish Flu—
17-50 million dead, bodies tucked away in
empty warehouses. How I worry my husband
will get sick, my sister, daughter, grandchildren.
The stories that begin with sickness gloss over
whom the virus takes. I stand outside at dusk—
cumulonimbus pinking to peach, settling on gray.
It is the way of things the ancient stories say—
we all become dust again and return to the stars.

UNIVERSE
by Abbe Rolnick

If I could, I'd wrap my arms around each of you.
I'd protect you from the worries of the world
But I am the world.
Each step you take leaves an imprint.
Each of your fears comes from the unknown.
I can't see beyond this galaxy,
To know what is next.
If I could, I'd leap forward into the future
To lead the way.
But you are my future.
I need your wisdom,
Careful use of my resources.
Show me your heart.
I will give you my soul.
I am your world.
You are my stars.

BIOGRAPHICAL NOTES

BRENDA M. ASTERINO graduated from Stephens College with an AA in Humanities. She also earned a BS in Biology from Finley College, Ohio, and masters degrees from Ohio State University and the Ohio Academy of Holistic Health. Other areas of study and teachers include Atlantic University; Lori Williams; Lively Stones Fellowship; Patricia Mischel. Presently, she is involved in energy work, as a radio producer participating in ham radio with San Juan County Amateur Radio Society, and the American Red Cross as a volunteer. Living on Lopez Island, she loves spending time with her daughter, son-in-law, and grandchildren.

Born and raised in Lebanon, **NADIA BOULOS** moved to the United States in 2001 where she now resides with her husband and two children. A graduate of Western Washington University, with a bachelor's degree in business marketing, she worked as a Marketing Manager in Bellingham for four years. More recently, she started her own web design company, Reset Web Design. Her childhood was marked by the traumatizing experience of the Lebanese civil war. This is reflected in her poetry and short stories. She enjoys yoga, hiking, playing music, traveling, and of course, spending time with her family.

NANCY CANYON has been published in *True Stories II*; *Memory into Memoir*; *Take a Stand, Art Against Hate*; *Water~Stone Review*; *Fourth Genre*; *Floating Bridge Review*; *Able Muse*; *Main Street Rag*; *Clover*; and more. With an MFA in Creative Writing from Pacific Lutheran University and a Certificate in Fiction from the University of Washington, she teaches for Chuckanut Writers and coaches for The Narrative Project. Ms. Canyon won the Cygnus Award for Paranormal Fiction for *Celia's Heaven*, her recent novel. *Saltwater*, a book of poetry and *Celia's Heaven* are available through villagebooks.com. Her memoir, "Struck," is forthcoming. More at www.nancycanyon.com.

ISABEL CASTRO is a first generation Costa Rican-American. She received a BA in Liberal Studies-Elementary Education from Humboldt State University and has taught and led therapeutic programs for all ages, from preschoolers to seniors. After traveling the world exploring organic farms, sustainable living, permaculture, indigenous cultures, and herbal medicine, she saw that Ayurveda distilled the core of her findings into a complete, holistic health science. In 2012 she became an Ayurvedic Health Practitioner and Yoga Instructor. Today she leads groups, demystifying health, and making it an approachable daily practice to promote health in body, mind, and spirit.

SUSAN CHASE-FOSTER has written poems in her backyard cottage on the Salish Sea, in coffee cafés in Alaska, teahouses clinging to mountains above Taipei, and with her feet in the hot sands of New Zealand's beaches. Her poems have been published in numerous anthologies, most recently in *Alaska Women Speak*, *Heron Clan VII*, and *Cirque*. She is the author of *XieXie Taipei*, a collection of poems written in Taiwan. Susan believes that writing poetry during this pandemic and wearing a mask in public are keeping her, and many others, alive.

LISA DAILEY is an avid traveler and writer. She is currently putting the final touches on her memoir, "Square Up," detailing the adventures and misadventures of a seven-month trip around the world as well as her own personal journey through grief. In her time abroad, she unearthed new ways of looking at her life through her discoveries in remote corners of the world and continues to enrich her life through travel. A native Montanan, Lisa makes her home by the ocean in Bellingham, Washington, but returns to her roots every summer for a healthy dose of mountains and Big Sky.

VICTORIA DOERPER lives in Bellingham and writes poetry and creative nonfiction. Her work appears in several literary publications, including *Cirque, Clover, Bindweed,* and *The Plum Tree Tavern*. Other publications include the anthology *For Love of Orcas* and *Orion Magazine*. Her first book of poetry, *What If We All Bloomed? Poems of Nature, Love, and Aging* was published in October 2019. During these pandemic times, she finds solace in long walks, where she learns lessons from the wild beings whose paths she shares.

Poetry is new to **MARIAN EXALL**. After a career as an employment lawyer, she turned to writing fiction, including the *Sarah McKinney Mysteries* series. Exall was born and raised in the UK, and lived in France and Belgium before emigrating to the US Since moving to the Pacific Northwest in 2006, and especially during this pandemic, she finds her inspiration and comfort in the natural beauty around us, and the warm community of writers. For more information: www.marianexall.com.

SUSAN E. GREISEN is a poet, author, and photographer who finds stories, messages, and images from her one-room grade school in Nebraska, to the rainforests in Africa, to the mountain tops in Tibet. Susan received her BS in Nursing at San Francisco State University and worked abroad for Peace Corps and CARE. Over the years she journeyed to over forty countries on six continents. Susan's awareness of diverse people and cultures with her eye for detail is what makes her writing and photography come alive. Her memoir, *In Search of Pink Flamingos,* was released in April 2020. Find details at susangreisen.com.

MARY LOU HABERMAN, a sojourner, finds sanctuary when penning memoir, family stories, poems, and essays. She spends time putzing, pondering, playing piano, and learning Spanish. Her upcoming memoir weaves her life search for peace while living with bipolar disorder with the journey of women who came before her. Her story, "The Marlboro Man," was published by The Narrative Project in *True Stories, Volume II.*

LAURA KALPAKIAN is the author of sixteen novels and four collections of short fiction under her own name, books published in the USA and the UK. Most recently, *The Great Pretenders* appeared in 2019. Her first nonfiction book, *Memory Into Memoir* will be published by the University of New Mexico Press, Fall 2021. She is a co-founder of Red Wheelbarrow Writers.

LINDA LAMBERT—The OED's definition of lambert, n.—"a unit of luminance (brightness),"—suggests a personal mission statement for writers: to use a flashlight of lively words to bring illumination to a subject. Her chosen genres are creative nonfiction and poetry, plus the occasional blog post at lindaQlambert.com and cookingwithchala.com. She is a retired librarian, a genealogy buff, a happy member of two critique groups, and genetically unrelated to the German physicist and polymath Johann Heinrich Lambert (1728-1777) whose name bears his discovery and was her prompt for this dictionary dalliance.

During the pandemic, **SHANNON LAWS** continues to work at two essential jobs, claiming she will need a vacation once this is all over. After discovering a taste for poetry twelve years ago, she just can't seem to quit the habit. Her latest book is an audiobook of satire poems titled *You Love Me, You Love Me Not* published in 2019 by Amazon, Audible, and Bandcamp. Shannon makes her home in Bellingham, Washington.

DICK LITTLE is a retired attorney and government lobbyist who has lived in Bellingham for forty years. His writing has been published in the *Seattle Times*, the *Seattle Post-Intelligencer*; and the *Santa Fe Writers Project*. His work has also appeared in *Cirque Magazine, Clover, A Literary Rag*, and *So Much Depends Upon*, an anthology by Red Wheelbarrow Writers. Dick is the author of two short story collections, *Postcards from the Road*, and *Jakey's Fork – A River's Journey*, and also the novel *City Haul*. More of his writing can be found at "The Write Stuff," http://pepys2000.blogspot.com.

REBECCA MABANGLO-MAYOR'S nonfiction, poetry, and short fiction have appeared in print and online in several journals and anthologies. Her poetry chapbook *Pause Mid-Flight* was released in 2010. She is a co-editor of *True Stories: The Narrative Project Vols. I, II* and *III*, and her poetry and essays have been collected in *Dancing Between Bamboo Poles*. She has performed as a storyteller since 2006 and specializes in stories based on Filipino folktales and Filipino-American history. Rebecca received her MFA in Creative Writing from Pacific Lutheran University; BA in Humanities from WSU; and MA in English with honors from Western Washington University.

CAROL MCMILLAN is compelled to write by her unrelenting and incorrigible muse. Dr. McMillan has been published in academic journals; her short stories and poems appear in several anthologies. She is the author of one book, *White Water, Red Walls*, in which she uses poetry, photographs, and paintings to chronicle her rafting trip down the Grand Canyon. She is currently working on a memoir of her experiences during the 1960s in the San Francisco Bay Area.

KATE MILLER is a poet and teacher who has lived in Bellingham for more than twenty years. They love birds and dogs, though they prefer herding dogs to bird dogs. They are currently exploring their birth family through internet means but look forward to another trip to the Great Smokey Mountains after the pandemic. Poetry has been an important survival tool during these uncertain times.

As a Peace Corps volunteer in Kenya a few years back, **JENNIFER MULLER** traveled quite a bit. A lot of the places she has written about she has been to; a lot of them she hasn't. Rafting the Nile in Uganda, living in a Montana ghost town, African safaris, Mayan ruins, forts on the Ghana coast all fill her scrapbooks. She still travels in her head every time she writes, even if she doesn't get out as much as she wishes. She currently lives in the Pacific Northwest and looks forward to filling many more pages.

CHERYL NELSON is a retired preschool teacher who has lived in Bellingham, Washington, for three years. She attended Western Washington University where she completed her BA in Early Childhood Education. Cheryl has had the opportunity to travel and volunteer in several Central American countries. She loves the outdoors and enjoys spending time in Bellingham area parks with her dog, Mimi. Cheryl's poetry was chosen for the top 30 in the King County poetry on buses in 2016 and top 100 in 2017. She is grateful to have met so many gifted writers through RWB and The Narrative Project.

JOE NOLTING is grateful for family and friends—for each day on this planet—and finds joy in the written word, two-wheeled transportation, and watching anything with wings. He coordinates Kids Need Books (knbbellingham.org), providing free books to underserved families throughout Whatcom County. He believes everyone has a voice that needs to be heard.

JANET OAKLEY writes award-winning historical fiction, but occasionally strays into poetry when something from nature or her garden inspires her. Her writing has been recognized with a 2013 Bellingham Mayor's Arts Award, the Chanticleer Grand Prize for *Tree Soldier* and Goethe Grand Prize for *The Jøssing Affair*, the 2018 Will Rogers Silver Medallion and two WILLA Silver Awards. *Timber Rose* is the 2015 WILLA Award finalist. When not writing she enjoys working in her newly deer-proofed garden, a hike in the woods, and the antics of her chickadees and Barney, the Berwick wren.

CAMI OSTMAN is the author of the memoir, *Second Wind: One Woman's Midlife Quest to Run Seven Marathons on Seven Continents* and the editor of several anthologies. Cami is one of the founders of Red Wheelbarrow Writers in Bellingham, Washington, and is the CEO of The Narrative Project, which supports writers in getting their books done.

PENNY PAGE is a writer, a reader, a gardener, and a native Bellinghamster. She writes primarily paranormal mysteries, which include her self-published novella *Not Haunted*, and three other novels: *Coven Corners* (a PNWA Sci/Fi Paranormal finalist), *Bayview Cemetery*, and *A New Kind of Monster*.

C.J. PRINCE hails from Lemuria. In recent years, Prince documented biodiversity in the Sasquatch Nation. Settled with pen and ink and a handful of paint brushes, Prince makes redacted sentences and starlight paintings in a forest cave, wearing red wheel shoes.

LAURA RINK is pursuing her MFA in creative writing at the Rainier Writing Workshop at Pacific Lutheran University in Tacoma, Washington. For her creative thesis, she is researching and writing about her Armenian family and the 1915 Armenian genocide. For her critical paper, she is exploring how authors write into silence—the private silence of untold stories and the public silence of suppressed stories. She lives in Bellingham, Washington, with her husband and their Tortico dog-cat, Sliver. She occasionally blogs at LauraRink.com.

DRUE (BeDo) ROBINSON is an award-winning playwright, director, and theatre practitioner whose adaptation of Lysistrata (published at playscripts.com) was performed in 400+ places around the globe after 9/11. She received an MFA from Columbia University's School of the Arts in New York City, has taught performance, writing, oral history, trial law, and public speaking to students of all ages, and was the Founder and Artistic Director of Bellingham Children's Theatre for over fifteen years. She has climbed Katahdin barefoot, ridden her bicycle around Greece, and taught nuns to juggle in Italy. She is forever intrigued by that one bird in a line of twenty sitting just a little farther away from the others, and is awed by the power of a comma.

ABBE ROLNICK grew up in the suburbs of Baltimore, Maryland. Her first major cultural jolt occurred at age fifteen when her family moved to Miami Beach, Florida. After attending Boston University, she lived in Puerto Rico, where she owned a bookstore. Her writings include: *River of Angels*, *Color of Lies*, and *Founding Stones* novels in the *Generation of Secrets* series, as well as *Cocoon of Cancer: An Invitation to Love Deeply,* and *Tattle Tales: Essays and Stories Along the Way*. Abbe lives with her husband, Jim, amid twenty acres in Skagit Valley, Washington. Visit her website: www.abberolnick.com.

BETTY SCOTT writes...re-visions...and rewrites: stories, essays, and poems. They ask: "How does the spirit stay alive, seduced and unrealized?" Her answers come from a devotion to family and friends, gratitude for the bountiful sights and flavors of Mother Earth, and a passion for the tones of meditative practices. She appreciates the community of Red Wheelbarrow Writers for their mastery of skills, support, and companionship through these difficult times. Scott's book, *Central Heating: Poems that Celebrate Love, Loss and Planet Earth*, published by Cave Moon Press, can be purchased at Village Books or by contacting: betty@bettyscottwriter.com.

ELIZABETH SCOTT TERVO is a novelist and poet. Her memoir, *The Sun Does Not Shine Without You*, set at the end of the Soviet period, is forthcoming in the Republic of Georgia, and her poetry has appeared or is slated to appear in *St. Katherine's Review*, *The Basilian Journal*, and *Eye to the Telescope*. A short story related to the memoir appears in the *New Haven Review*, and another story in *Ham Lit*. She is co-coordinator of the Doxacon Seattle writers' group for Christianity and Speculative Literature, and is a Presbytera, or Greek Orthodox priest's wife.

JUDY SHANTZ is an aspiring writer living in Bellingham, Washington. She writes primarily for her own pleasure, finding in writing both a joy and an avocation. Her first love is fiction, especially historical fiction. However, in the last few years she has felt encouraged to try her hand at essay, memoir, and now, for the first time, poetry.

JK SMALL is a writer, a health care provider, a parent, a grandparent, and has many interests and hobbies. Poetry comforts JK during dark periods in life. Writing, reading, or listening to poetry—whether silly or serious—heals the heart. JK resides in Bellingham to be close to family and enjoy the natural beauty of the Pacific Northwest. It has been an added bonus to be included in the thriving writing community of Bellingham. Thank you, Red Wheelbarrow Writers, for your commitment to writers everywhere—especially during the COVID pandemic.

GARY WADE was born and raised in southern Iowa, then educated there and in the wider world. His life experiences include farming, factory and laboratory work, service in the US Air Force, and pursuits as a photographer, ecologist, scientist, teacher, father, and grandfather. Now a refugee from corn fields and technical writing, he has lived in Bellingham by choice since 2005. Gary's poetry has appeared in *Clover, A Literary Rag*, and a number of anthologies. Until a certain virus appeared, he was a regular performance poet at several regional live venues.

JEAN WAIGHT writes about family, American society, and the pleasures of sustainable food. Her work has appeared in the Red Wheelbarrow Writers anthology *Memory into Memoir*, in *Cirque: A Literary Journal for the North Pacific Rim*, in *Ruminate Magazine, Whatcom Watch, The Bellingham Herald,* and kaminea.com. Her research appeared in *Research in Social Stratification and Mobility*. She has an MA in Sociology and formerly worked in management and communications. She recently completed a book manuscript about finding a religious revolution in a progressive church. She and her husband live in Bellingham, Washington. Find more at jeanwaight.com.

J. L. WRIGHT has two published poetry books: *Unadoptable Joy* and *Homeless Joy*. Her poems have appeared in *Taj Mahal Review, GNU Journal, Solstice* and nearly a dozen anthologies. She has been an active member of Red Wheelbarrow Writers, Whatcom Peace and Justice Writers, and Village Books Writing Groups. She will be recognized this fall with a Sue Boynton Merit Award.

ACKNOWLEDGMENTS

Red Wheelbarrow Writers...you are the creators who come together monthly to share stories, create collaborative tales, and encourage novice and seasoned writers alike. Most importantly, you are the poets who made this book possible by your involvement in every step of the journey.

Thank you to those members who lobbied for an anthology of strictly poetry. We are all pleased that so many writers who don't consider themselves to be poets stepped outside their comfort zones and dove into the world of poetry. We want to offer a special thanks to the faithful poets who started us off during April's National Poetry Writing Month and who kept writing the poetry that soothed and expressed our hearts long after April was over. Among those contributing more than half of the days in April to the Facebook group (some posting daily) are: Rebecca Mabanglo-Mayor, Joy Wright, C.J. Prince, Susan Chase-Foster, Victoria Doerper, and Joe Nolting.

Susan, Victoria, and Joe went above and beyond the writing of poetry to offer the rest of us support and editing for this volume. Without them, this book would not exist.

An additional enormous thank you goes to the following members for significant contribution to this volume:
- Laura Kalpakian, Cami Ostman, and Susan Tive for the concept of our community.
- Marian Exall and Drue (BeDo) Robinson for proofreading.
- Drue (Be Do) Robinson, also, for penning the words "this uncommon solitude," in the poem *Hands I*, which became our title.
- Lisa Dailey for being our technical guru and our publisher with her wonderful Sidekick Press.

Thanks also to the many locations that have housed our monthly gatherings and for the technology of Zoom which has allowed us to continue to meet even in the middle of a global pandemic. Deepest heartfelt thanks to the wonderful team at Village Books, and especially Paul Hanson, for ongoing support and cheerleading of writers in our greater community.

And finally, grateful thanks to cover designer, Serge Solomenko of Spoken Designs.